Learn Italian Like a Native
for Beginners - Level 1

Learning Italian in Your Car Has Never Been Easier! Have Fun with Crazy Vocabulary, Daily Used Phrases, Exercises & Correct Pronunciations

www.LearnLikeNatives.com

© Copyright 2020 By Learn Like A Native

ALL RIGHTS RESERVED

No part of this book may be reproduced, stored in a retrieval system, or transmitted in any form or by any means, without the prior written permission of the publisher.

Table of Contents

INTRODUCTION 1

WHY LEARN ITALIAN IS, A GOOD CHOICE 5

CHAPTER 1 – THE FIRST IMPRESSION IS VERY IMPORTANT 11

CHAPTER 2 – ARE WE RELATED? 22

CHAPTER 3 – WHAT DAY IS IT? 30

CHAPTER 4 – THERE IS NO GIFT LIKE THE PRESENT. 42

CHAPTER 5 – HAVE A LOOK AROUND 55

CHAPTER 6 – HOW FAR CAN YOU COUNT? 64

CHAPTER 7 – WHAT DID YOU WANT TO BE WHEN YOU GREW UP? 73

CHAPTER 8 – WHERE ARE WE GOING? 84

CHAPTER 9 – SURVIVAL 101 91

CHAPTER 10 – WHAT IS THE COLOR OF THE SKY? 97

CHAPTER 11 – SO MUCH TO DO, SO MUCH TO SEE 103

CHAPTER 12 – I AM A BIT HUNGRY 113

CONCLUSION 126

Introduction

If you have always wanted to learn Italian, you are not alone. According to the most recent statistics, Italian is the fourth most studied language in the world, with more and more people getting seduced by the language and its culture every single day.

Art, history, fashion, and design are just few of the reasons to study this beautiful, melodic language.

There is no right way to learn a new language. With so many options available, it is not surprising you might feel overwhelmed when choosing a learning style or method!

You probably have many questions; maybe you have no idea even where to start, and you are wondering if it's worth it. Well, I can guarantee you that learning Italian it's more than worth the effort! We will be right here to help and support you in this adventure and, thanks to the right tools and technology, your efforts will pay off quickly.

According to researches and studies conducted on people who speak and study Italian as non-native, the best and fastest way to learn this language is not to study grammar (as you may have guessed). Instead, it is much useful to study, recognize, and use selected keywords in everyday life and to reinforce your vocabulary through guided discussions and conversations.

Learning a new language is a long, gradual process. It is a far too big task to tackle all at once, and therefore we have broken it down into a series of lessons.

Multiple skills, as well as patience, are required to learn how to speak confidently and fluently, write a text to a friend, or watch an Italian TV series.

Most people who have only studied Italian through grammar books often struggle to speak the language in real life. Thanks to my method, you will speedily progress and feel more confident speaking Italian with a native.

In the audiobook format, the lessons are narrated by an Italian native speaker, so you can also grasp the proper diction while learning the language. Learn Italian by completing a series of interactive lessons: you won't just passively listen, but you will be encouraged to speak, repeat and perfect your pronunciation by comparing with native speakers. Thanks to the audiobook and its PDF version attached, you will be able to both train your ears or read and learn the spelling.

The best thing about this book is by far the flexibility it gives you to learn whenever and wherever you want! Our bite-sized lessons take roughly 20 to 30 minutes to complete and can be squeezed into your already busy schedule, whether you're sitting in your car or waiting for dinner to be ready.

With this book, you can choose the topic that is more relevant to you and your interests. Are you about to go on holiday? Look at the section dedicated to travel. Do you need to refresh your Italian for an upcoming business meeting? Our lessons have you covered: you can learn Italian anytime, anywhere.

What is the use of learning a new language and then forget it because you never get to use it in real life? For this reason, this book has been optimized to help you retain as much information as possible. Take advantage of micro-learning. You can start to practice what you will learn in our lessons: writing, listening, and speaking.

www.LearnLikeNatives.com

The goal of learning any language is to be able to converse with native speakers. Therefore, a book for language learning should allow you to achieve this objective. While it is surely important to practice with discipline and devotion, to succeed, you will also need an effective plan to help you along the way.

Fortunately, this book has been studied by capable language experts, educators, and designers who know everything you need to make the most of learning a new language. We guaranteed a high-quality Italian learning experience that is interesting, and yes, even fun...!

Why Learn Italian is, a good choice

First of all, studies and researches show that learning a new language is a really good exercise for your brain and helps to improve your memory.

Italian is the fourth most studied language in the whole world, with more and more people getting seduced every single day. This is not surprising, considering its link to art, culture, fashion, and food just to name a few.

Wanting to travel to Italy is definitely one of the main reasons why people decide to learn Italian. Italy is one of the most beautiful and historically rich places in the world and, according to UNESCO, most of the world's cultural heritage sites are here located.

Learning a new language should always be about communication. The best way to make any experience abroad truly memorable is to speak a bit of the local language. By doing so, you will be able to communicate with the locals and create deeper connections. Speaking the same language means you can understand each other better. And trust me, this is going to make the time you spend away much easier and, more importantly, it will give you the chance to really immerse yourself in another culture.

Another thing to consider is that nowadays, every place is filled with Italian restaurants. Learning Italian will give you the chance to understand better their culinary tradition better and – more importantly – what you are eating. For example, did you know that there is a kind of pasta called "farfalle", which literally translates to "butterflies"?

And how can we forget the musicality and the charm of its words? It is a melodic language. A real pleasure to listen to!

You would also be pleased to know that Italian is much easier to learn than other languages. There are no silent letters or missing sounds and it is a completely phonetic language. This means that, once you know the alphabet and learn a few rules, you will be able to read and perfectly pronounce every single word. Moreover, as both English and Italian have Latin roots, some of the words and sounds are either the same or very similar. That's just amazing, right?

If you are a lover of classical music, you will surely know that many operas were composed in Italian. Just think about Giuseppe Verdi or Giacomo Puccini.

Or maybe you are passionate about fashion and have always dreamed of going to Milan's fashion week. In Italy, you will find the most prestigious fashion houses, like Armani, Dolce & Gabbana, Prada, and Versace, to name a few.

Whatever is your reason or motivation to learn Italian, we will be with you every step of the way.

www.LearnLikeNatives.com

FREE BOOK!

Get the *FREE BOOK* that reveals the secrets path to learn any language fast, and without leaving your country.

Discover:

- The **language 5 golden rules** to master languages at will

- Proven **mind training techniques** to revolutionize your learning

- A complete step-by-step guide to **conquering any language**

www.LearnLikeNatives.com

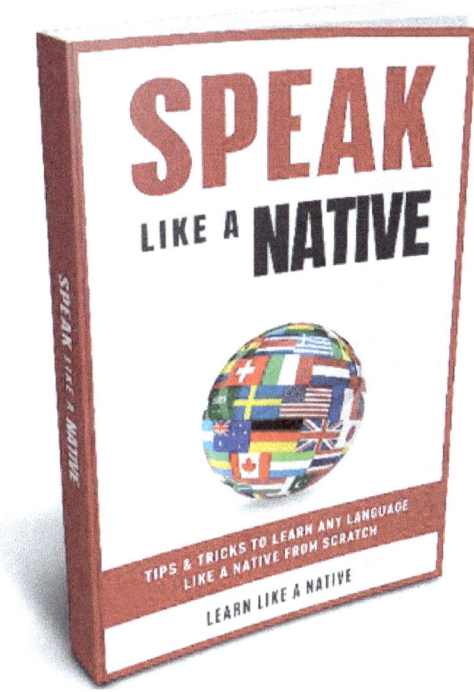

www.LearnLikeNatives.com

Chapter 1 – The first impression is very important

Everyone knows the old saying, "you only get one chance to make a first impression".

Therefore, it's no surprise that one of the first things every child learns is to say hello and introduce themselves. Even J.K. Rowling, the famous author of that young wizard's adventures, said "A good first impression can work wonders", and I completely agree.

Just a simple "Hello" can make all the difference in a conversation. That's exactly the reason why we will begin this exciting adventure with the Italian greetings. You will learn how to introduce yourself and greet people at different times of the day, among other useful things.

We will start with the most popular greetings. There are several ways to greet people in Italian, depending on who you are addressing and whether you want to be formal or not.

Ready to start? I really hope you are as excited as I am!

So, let's begin with the most common ways to greet someone in Italian:

Hello.	Ciao

Chow

The word "Ciao" is probably one of the most popular Italian words, now used as a friendly salutation around the world. It is an informal greeting that can be used at any time of the day for both "Hello" and "Goodbye". It is considered highly informal and used among people who already know each other pretty well.

Least known but very useful is another salutation:

Hello.	Salve

Sahl-veh

When you are unsure of how to greet people, it is better to use this formal version for "Hello". It comes from Latin, meaning 'to be well'. More polite than "ciao", it is preferable to use between colleagues or strangers.

| Good morning. | Buongiorno |

Bwohn-johr-noh

Literally translated "Buongiorno" means "good day". It's slightly more formal and common between strangers, but it would not be a problem if you use this to greet someone you already know. It is also used as a greeting upon waking up. You can use it both in the morning and in the afternoon.

As in English, also in Italian the greetings change depending on the time of the day. As such, in the afternoon, you can switch to:

| Good afternoon. | Buon pomeriggio |

Bwohn poh-meh-rih-joh

"Buon pomeriggio" (Good afternoon) exists in Italian. However, it would sound a bit odd if you greeted people saying this as it is not that common. Generally, native speakers will keep using "Buongiorno" also in the afternoon.

As the afternoon sets in, you should say "Good evening".

| Good evening. | Buona sera |

Bwoh-nah-seh-rah

You can use this greeting on both formal and informal occasions, but remember that it is only used when you are arriving.

Finally, when it's bedtime, you will say:

| Good night. | Buona notte |

Bwoh-nah-noht-teh

Remember! You should use "Buona notte" only when you are saying goodbye late at night and, as such, implying that you or your party are going to bed. It is also used to wish sweet dreams.

Last one. When departing you can simply use "Ciao" or the more polite salutation for Goodbye:

| Goodbye. | Arrivederci |

Ahr-ree-veh-dehr-chee

As for Goodbye, you can use both "Ciao" or "Arrivederci" (recommended for more formal occasions). It is similar to the word "aloha". As you may know, Hawaiians only use one word for both "hello" and "goodbye", which is "aloha". In a similar way, also in Italian most greetings can be used for both hello and goodbye.

You should also remember that, depending on whether you are greeting a friend or a stranger, you would use a different salutation.

For example, when entering a restaurant in the evening (or in any other formal occasion), you will say "Buona sera" if you want to sound polite. Although you can use "Ciao" if you are meeting some old friends or greeting someone you already know (informal occasion).

| Farewell. | Addio. |
| **Farewell**. I love you. | **Addio**. Ti amo. |

Ah-dee-oh

"Addio" is used as a final salutation when you are pretty sure you are not going to see someone ever again. It's a phrase very rich in drama, sadness, or irony, depending on the cases.

There is also a more informal version of "Arrivederci":

| See you later. | Ci vediamo |
| Great! **See you later.** | Perfetto! **Ci vediamo.** |

Cee veh-dihah-moh

How is your pronunciation? I hope you are starting to make progress.

See you in a few.	Ci vediamo più tardi
Ok! See you in a few.	Okl! **Ci vediamo** più tardi.

Cee veh-dihah-moh pihyou tahr-dee

When greeting, you may also want to ask how someone is doing.

How are you?	Come stai?

Koh-meh-stahy

You may have noticed that there is no literal translation, and the word "you" is not translated. While in English the pronoun is always used, in Italian the ending of the verb usually makes it clear who the subject is, so no pronoun is necessary.

Asking "Come stai?" is a really good way to start a friendly conversation. It is an informal greeting and can also be used between people you are familiar with to ask about their health or mood.

How can I help you?	Come posso aiutarti?

Koh-meh poos-soh ah-you-tahr-the

At this point, you have probably figured out the connection between two words: "how" and "come", and you know how important this word is in any language. Let's see another sentence that uses the word "Come":

| What is your name? | Come ti chiami? |

Koh-meh tee kyah-mee

To say what your name is in Italian you use:

| My name is | Mi chiamo |
| **My name is** John. | **Mi chiamo** John. |

Meek kyah-moh

| I am | Io sono |
| **I am** new around here. | **Io sono nuovo** da queste parti. |

Ih-oh Soh-noh

| Thanks/Thank you. | Grazie. |

Grah-tzee

"Grazie" is used to say both "thanks" or "thank you". However, if you wish to show more gratitude, you could say "many thanks," which translates to "Grazie mille" (literally a thousand thank yous).

Grah-tzee mih-leh

| I am sorry. | Mi dispiace. |

Mee dees-pyah-cheh

| Nice to see you again. | Piacere di rivederti. |

Pyah-cheh-reh dee ree-veh-dehr-tee

Was it too hard? Don't worry. Greetings are basic phrases you will need to memorize, but I promise that the upcoming sentences will be shorter and easier to remember.

| What is new? | Che novità ci sono? |

Che noh-vee-tah cee soh-noh

Another sentence with a similar meaning is "Cosa mi racconti?" What do you say?

Koh-sah mee rahc-chon-tee

| How are you doing? | Come va? |

Koh-meh vah

As you might know, "Ok" is an English expression. Nevertheless, it's universally used worldwide, even among Italian speakers. You should be aware, however, that there is an Italian equivalent as well:

| Ok. | Va bene. |

Vah beh-neh

How is it going? Are you finding it difficult, or is it easy? Maybe you need to practice a little bit more. Remember: practice is the key to mastery! Anyway, before we move to another topic, let's take a look at a short conversation that uses some of the words we have just learned.

Vendor   *Good morning!*

(Rivenditore):   Buongiorno.

John: *Good morning to you, too.*

             Buongiorno anche a te.

Vendor: *How can I help you?*

             Come posso aiutarti?

John: *I am here to pick up a cake.*

             Sono qui per ritirare una torta.

Vendor: *Sure. What is your name?*

             Certamente. Come ti chiami?

John: *My name is John Hill.*

             Mi chiamo John Hill.

Vendor: *Oh, I am sorry. Your bday cake is not ready yet.*

             Oh, mi dispiace. La tua torta di compleanno non è ancora pronta.

John: *Ok. When can I come pick it up?*

             Va bene. Quando posso venire a ritirarla?

Vendor: *It will be ready in one hour.*

	Sarà pronta in un'ora.
John:	*Great. I will run some errands and come back.*
	Fantastico. Vado a fare delle commisioni e torno.
Vendor:	*Thanks for understanding. See you in a few.*
	Grazie per la comprensione. Ci vediamo più tardi.
John:	*Sure. See you later!*
	Certo. A più tardi!

I hope you are not getting low blood sugar, because you will have to wait for a while. In the meantime, shall we go and learn some new words and phrases that relate to family and relatives? This could be really handy if you are going to have a birthday party!

Chapter 2 – Are we related?

I am sure your family would be pleased to tell you the story of your first word.

Language acquisition starts with receptive language, the understanding of sounds and words of the world around us. There is a good chance that either "mum" or "dad" (or a variable of these) was the first word you learned.

Dad	Papá
My **dad** went out to buy milk.	Mio **papá** è uscito a comprare il latte.

Pah-pà

Accent marks are very important in the Italian language. They can seem insignificant, but those tiny marks can completely change the meaning of a word. The accent on the à in "papà" - short on the first syllable and hard accent on the second - is fundamental as without it, you would be referring to the Pope (Papa).

Mom	Mamma
My **mom** is there, by the door.	Mia **mamma** è lì, vicino alla porta.

Mahm-mah

Son	Figlio
My **son** used to play tennis.	Mio **figlio** giocava a tennis.

Fee-glee-oh

Daughter	Figlia
My **daughter** likes to dance.	A mia **figlia** piace ballare.

Fee-glee-ah

In Italian, there are two genders: every noun must be either masculine or feminine. Figlio/Figlia is a good example. As an introductory guide, it is good to know that singular:

- Nouns ending in "o" are masculine (male), with few exceptions;
- Nouns ending in "a" are nearly all feminine (female).

Throughout this book, we will see several examples of these. As a general rule, you can form the feminine or masculine version of nouns changing the final vowel.

Therefore, you would use words like "figlia" or "questa" for female, and "figlio" or "questo" for male.

Brother	Fratello
This is my **brother** Alberto.	Questo è mio **fratello** Alberto.

Frah-teh-loh

Sister	Sorella
She is my **sister** Carla.	Lei è mia **sorella** Carla.

Soh-reh-lah

Uncle	Zio

| I have two **uncles**. | Io ho due **zii**. |

Zee-oh

| Aunt | Zia |
| My **aunt** has two kids. | Mia **zia** ha due figli. |

Zee-ah

While in English you can simply form the plurals by adding "s" at the end of every word, different rules apply in Italian. First of all, it is important to know the gender of the word: masculine or feminine. Then, to turn a singular word into a plural one, you usually need to change the final vowel as it follows:

- For nouns ending in "o" you will need to change the ending to "i" (Example: Zio – Zii)
- For nouns ending in "a" you will need to change the ending to "e" (Example: Zia –Zie)

But be careful, as there are some exceptions!

| Cousin | Cugino |

| My **cousin** lives far away from here. | Mio **cugino** vive lontano da qui. |

Cooh-jee-noh

| Grandfather | Nonno |
| My **grandfather** has a good memory | Mio **nonno** ha una buona memoria. |

Noh-noh

| Grandmother | Nonna |
| My **grandmother** loved knitting. | Mia **nonna** amava lavorare a maglia. |

Noh-nah

How is it going so far? Don't you worry, we just need to meet a few more people, and then we can take a short break.

| Siblings | Fratello/Sorella |
| I have three **siblings**. | Io ho tre **fratelli/sorelle**. |

Frah-teh-loh/Soh-reh-lah

Relatives	Parenti
I have many **relatives**.	Io ho molti **parenti**.

Pah-rehn-tee

Family	Famiglia
My **family** is big.	La mia è una **famiglia** numerosa.

Fah-mih-lih-ah

Neighbor	Vicino
Dan is a great **neighbor**.	Dan è un buon **vicino.**

Vee-cee-noh

Are you ready to use those words you have just learned? Great!

Allyson: *Happy birthday!*

Buon compleanno!

Kelly: *Hello! Thanks a lot! I am happy that you came.*

Ciao! Grazie mille! Mi fa piacere tu sia venuta.

Allyson: I am happy that you invited me.

Sono felice che tu mi abbia invitata.

Kelly: Sure. Let me show you who everyone is.

Certo. Lascia che ti mostri chi sono tutti.

Allyson: Great!

Fantastico!

Kelly: That girl is my sister, and my cousin John is sitting next to her.

Quella ragazza è mia sorella, e quello seduto di fianco a lei è mio cugino John.

Allyson: Yeah. Next to them is your brother Mark, right?

Si. Accanto a loro c'è tuo fratello Mark, giusto?

Kelly: Perfect! Yes. He picks me up sometimes.

Esatto! Si. A volte mi viene a prendere.

Allyson: I remember.

Me lo ricordo.

Kelly: Good. By that other corner are grandma, grandpa, and uncle Ed.

Bene. All'altro angolo ci sono nonna, nonno e zio Ed.

Allyson: *Your grandma looks so young!*

Tua nonna sembra così giovane!

Kelly: *Yes. I hope I have the same luck.*

Si. Spero avrò la stessa fortuna.

Allyson: *Don't we all?*

Non è quello che speriamo tutti?

Kelly: *Let's see… who's missing? Oh, well. Dad is outside, with the neighbors and the rest of the family.*

Vediamo… chi manca? Oh, ecco. Papá è fuori, con i vicini e il resto della famiglia.

Allyson: *Great! I can't wait to meet them.*

Ottimo! Non vedo l'ora di conoscerlo.

So, what do you think? Learning a new language is about listening to things over and over again and repeating many times. My advice is to always say the words out loud. This is an excellent way to practice a new language and, if you do so, you will see a significant improvement in the next chapters.

Chapter 3 – What day is it?

Learn how to measure and tell the time is hugely valuable. In many cultures, punctuality is extremely important and viewed as a form of respect, and I personally think it is a great sign of courtesy. Of course, you will also learn the days of the week and months, so you can make plans. Another thing you may want to know before leaving for a foreign country is what season is it, to know what to pack and dress accordingly.

As always, we will start with the basics:

Second	Secondo / Secondi
One minute has sixty **seconds**.	Un minuto ha sessanta **secondi**.

Seh-cohn-doh / Seh-cohn-dee

Minute	Minuto / Minuti
One hour has sixty **minutes**.	Un'ora ha sessanta **minuti**.

Mee-noo-toh / Mee-noo-tee

Hour	Ora / Ore
There are twenty-four **hours** in a day.	Ci sono ventiquattro **ore** in un giorno.

Oh-rah / Oh-reh

Great, let's carry on.

Day	Giorno / Giorni
April has thirty **days**.	Aprile ha trenta **giorni**.

Jorh-noh / Jorh-nee

Week	Settimana / Settimane
We have one **week** to finish.	Finiamo tra una **settimana**.

Seh-tee-mah-nah / Seh-tee-mah-neh

Month	Mese / Mesi
We will be there next **month**.	Saremo lì il **mese** prossimo.

Meh-seh / Meh-see

Year	Anno / Anni
One more birthday, one more **year**.	Un altro compleanno, un altro **anno**.

Ah-noh / Ah-nee

Decade	Decennio
This **decade** is going to end soon.	Questo **decennio** sta per finire.

Deh-chen-nioh

Century	Secolo
This is the discovery of the **century**.	Questa è la scoperta del **secolo**.

See-kol-oh

Morning	Mattina
The meeting was this **morning**.	La riunione era questa **mattina**.

Mah-tee-nah

Afternoon	Pomeriggio

| Will you be there in the **afternoon**? | Sarai lì nel **pomeriggio**? |

Poh-meh-ree-joh

| Night | Notte |
| Moon comes out at **night**. | Di **notte** c'è la luna. |

Noh-teh

| Spring | Primavera |
| Everything flowers in **spring**. | Tutto fiorisce in **primavera**. |

Pree-mah-veh-rah

Remember: the soft sound you need for "rah" will depend on the amount of air that you breathe out.

| Summer | Estate |
| We had a fun **summer**. | Abbiamo passato un'**estate** divertente. |

Ehs-tah-teh

| Autumn | Autunno |

| Look at the first **autumn** leaf. | Guarda le prime foglie d'**autunno**. |

How-tuh-noh

| Winter | Inverno |
| The **winter** is here. | E' arrivato l'**inverno**. |

In-vehr-noh

| January | Gennaio |
| **January** is the first month of the year. | **Gennaio** è il primo mese dell'anno. |

Jehn-nah-eeoh

At this point, you should know that, contrary to what happens in English, in Italian months and days of the week do not start with capital letters.

| February | Febbraio |
| That tree flowers in **February**. | Quell'albero fiorisce a **febbraio**. |

Feh-brah-yoh

March	Marzo
March is a good month for harvesting.	**Marzo** è un buon mese per il raccolto.

Marh-tzoh

April	Aprile
We stop activities on **April**.	Terminiamo le attività in **aprile**.

Ah-pree-leh

Have you noticed how most of the names of the months are similar between English and Italian? That's a relief, is it?

May	Maggio
May is going to be a great month.	**Maggio** sarà un mese fantastico.

Mah-joh

June	Giugno
The break starts on **June**.	Le vacanze iniziano a **giugno**.

Jooh-nyoh

July	Luglio
July is a hot month in Italy.	**Luglio** è un mese molto caldo in Italia.

Looh-lihoh

August	Agosto
This **August** will be rainy.	Questo **agosto** sarà piovoso.

Ah-goh-stoh

September	Settembre
Next semester starts in **September**.	Il prossimo semestre inizierà a **settembre**.

Seh-tehm-breh

October	Ottobre
We celebrated Halloween in **October**.	Noi festeggiamo Halloween in **ottobre**.

Oht-too-breh

November	Novembre

| My birthday is in **November**. | Il mio compleanno è a **novembre**. |

Noh-vehm-breh

| December | Dicembre |
| The year ends in **December**. | L'anno termina a **dicembre**. |

Dee-cehm-breh

| Monday | Lunedì |
| Today is **Monday**. | Oggi è **lunedì**. |

Loo-neh-dee

| Tuesday | Martedì |
| I have an appointment for next **Tuesday**. | Ho un appuntamento per **martedì** prossimo. |

Marh-teh-dee

Remember that the Italian "t" is pronounced very clear and strong, like the British one.

| Wednesday | Mercoledì |

Wednesday is not a good day for me.	Il **mercoledì** per me non è una bella giornata.

Mehr-ko-leh-dee

Thursday	Giovedì
I'll see you next **Thursday**.	Ci vediamo **giovedì** prossimo.

Joh-veh-dee

Friday	Venerdì
The party is next **Friday**.	La festa è **venerdì** prossimo.

Veh-nerh-dee

Please notice the grave accent mark on the words lunedì, martedì, mercoledì, giovedì, venerdì. The accent lets you know that, in these cases, the stress falls on the last syllable.

Saturday	Sabato
I play football every **Saturday**.	Io gioco a calcio ogni **Sabato**.

Sah-bah-toh

Sunday	Domenica
We can have breakfast this **Sunday**.	Possiamo fare colazione questa **Domenica**.

Doh-meh-nee-cah

How is it going? Are you ready for a short conversation?

Ally: *So, what are your plans for the next year?*

Quindi, che piani hai per il prossimo anno?

Juan: *I honestly don't know what will happen after the winter.*

Sinceramente non so cosa farò dopo l'inverno.

Ally: *Will you at least come back in February? The spring is lovely in here.*

Ma almeno ritornerai a febbraio? Qui la primavera è meravigliosa.

Juan: *If I don't, I promise I will be back to celebrate summer in July.*

Se non tornerò, prometto verrò per festeggiare l'estate a luglio.

Ally: *Everyone loves summer. I love autumn.*

Tutti amano l'estate. A me piace l'autunno.

Juan: *Why?*

Perchè?

Ally: *Leaves change colors, and I love the weather between September and November.*

Le foglie cambiano colore e amo il clima tra settembre e novembre.

Juan: *Two weeks ago, you didn't love it that much.*

Due settimane fa non ti piaceva così tanto.

Ally: *Are you talking of that rainy Wednesday? I hated that.*

Parli di quel mercoledì di pioggia? La odio.

Juan: *Yeah. And it's even worse when it rains on Mondays.*

Si. Ed è pure peggio quando piove di lunedì.

Ally: *Oh, sure. I don't like Mondays. I love Fridays.*

Oh, certo. Non mi piacciono i lunedì. Io amo i venerdì.

Juan: Like everyone. But I like Saturdays better.

Come tutti. Invece io preferisco i sabato.

Ally: Yes. Especially the ones in Spring, when you take your boat for a ride.

Si. Specialmente quelli in primavera, quando esci per un giro con la tua barca.

Juan: You remember it. Good.

Te lo ricordi. Brava.

It's not as hard as you thought, right? There is a lot to remember, but sometimes it's easier if you find the similarities between English and Italian, such as those in the names of the months. Again, practice makes perfect.

Now has come the time to learn some important verbs and how to conjugate them.

Chapter 4 – There is no gift like the Present

Just as in any other language, also in Italian verbs are an important part of everyday speaking. When studying a foreign language, the present is the first tense you will learn, as this will allow you to form simple sentences. It is used to describe something that is happening right now or a state of being. Using the present tense, you will be able to speak about your desires, interests, and plans.

First of all, in Italian, verb conjugation is done by changing the ending of the verb. Verbs are divided into 3 different categories, called "coniugazioni" - conjugations. Each one is characterized by a specific ending in its infinitive form:

- First conjugation: Verbs ending in -ARE (like amare)
- Second conjugation: Verbs ending in -ERE (like credere)
- Third conjugation: Verbs ending in -IRE (like partire)

In this chapter, I will teach you how to conjugate the regular verbs.

In addition, as you do in English, also in Italian you can merge all the 3rd person singular pronouns. For your convenience, this is what we will do here.

Hopefully, with a bit of practice, you will realize that Italian verb conjugation is actually much easier than it seems.

So, let's get started. There is no time like the present!

To love	**Amare**	**Root**	**Termination**
I love	Io amo	Am-	Are changes to "o"
You love	Tu ami		Are changes to "i"
He/She/It loves	Lui/Lei/Egli ama		Are changes to "a"
We love	Noi amiamo		Are changes to "iamo"
You love	Voi amate		Are changes to "ate"

| They love | Loro amano | | Are changes to "ano" |

The root of all regular verbs never changes. As you can see, the root is the part preceding the infinitive ending. So, for example, in "Amare" the root is "Am-". Like we said, the root always remains the same and different endings are added to denote the person, number or tense. Let's look at some examples.

I love the rain.	Io amo la pioggia.
She loves music.	Lei ama la musica.
You love movies.	Voi amate i film.
They love to play music.	Loro amano suonare.

Great! Here is a tip: using the above table, you will be able to conjugate every other regular verb that ends in "are". All you will have to do is add to the root the relevant ending, as we just did. Clearly, the same logic applies to the verbs of the second and third conjugation (-Ere and -Ire). That's good to know, right?

Here are a few more examples. For the verb "to sing" - "cantare", you can separate the root "Cant-", and all you will need to do is to add the correct ending, as previously explained. The root of the verb "to eat" – "mangiare" is "Mangi-", and for the verb "to share" - "condividere", the root is "Condivid-".

So, anyhow, what do you like to do in your free time? What are your interests? What are you passionate about? Come on, think about this for a moment. Verbs are important to discuss all of these things.

To believe	**Credere**	**Root**	**Termination**
I believe	Io credo		Ere changes to "o"
You believe	Tu credi	Cred-	Ere changes to "i"
He/She/It believes	Lui/Lei/Egli crede		Ere changes to "e"
We believe	Noi crediamo		Ere changes to "iamo"

You believe	Voi credete		Ere changes to "ete"
They believe	Loro credono		Ere changes to "ono"

You believe in loyalty.	Tu credi nella lealtà.
He only believes what is in front of his nose.	Lui crede solo a ciò che è davanti al suo naso.
You believe in yourselves.	Voi credete in voi stessi.
They believe in you.	Loro credono in te.

So, what have you learned, and what do you have faith in? Repeat with me: "io credo….". Eventually, you will be able to better express yourself in Italian, but –in the meantime- "io credo" is good enough.

Let's carry on with another important verb: "to leave" – "partire". In this case, the root is "Part-".

To leave	Partire	Root	Termination

I leave	Io parto		Ire changes to "o"
You leave	Tu parti		Ire changes to "i"
He/She/It leaves	Lei/Lui/Egli parte	Part-	Ire changes to "e"
We leave	Noi partiamo		Ire changes to "iamo"
You leave	Voi partite		Ire changes to "ite"
They leave	Loro partono		Ire changes to "ono"

I leave on a trip	Parto per un viaggio.
The train leaves at six.	Il treno parte alle sei.
We leave tomorrow.	Noi partiamo domani.

Now let's look at the present of the auxiliary verb "to be" – "essere". This verb is one of the most versatile, and you will use it a lot in Italian: to introduce yourself, find out more about something or someone, describe places and things, etc. It is an auxiliary verb and its purpose is to help other verbs conjugate in compound tenses. In other words, it helps to create more complex sentences and tenses.

There is also another verb that can sometimes be used with the same meaning of "to be": "stare" – "to stay". While in English "to stay" is only used to describe your location, in Italian, it can also be used to describe a state of being.

Here are some examples to explain the use of the verb "essere" (to be):

- To introduce yourself or describe something like nationality, profession, etc.: "You are Latin-American" -"Tu sei Latino Americano", "She is Lucy" –"Lei è Lucy", "I am a doctor" – "Io sono un medico"
- To describe something or someone. For example, "He is tall" – "Lui è alto", or "They are smart" – "Loro sono intelligenti".
- To speak about time and date, like "The meeting will be at seven" –"La riunione è alle sette", or "The dinner is ready" –"La cena è pronta".
- To talk about seasons and weather. For example "It is summer" –"E' estate".

Similarly, let's see when we should use the verb "stare" (to stay):

- To say or ask how someone is: "How are you?" – "Come stai?", "I'm fine" – "Sto bene".
- To give an order or exhortation: "Stay calm" – "Stai tranquillo".
- To explain where something is situated. "The house is on top of the mountain" –"La casa sta in cima alla montagna".
- To make continuous tenses or indicate an action. "I am studying" – "Sto studiando".

I know it may sound a bit confusing, but once you understand the differences, you will soon see how easy these are to use and how helpful they are to express yourself.

For the time being, let's see how to conjugate them.

To be	Essere	To stay	Stare	
I am	Io sono	I stay	Io sto	
You are	Tu sei	You stay	Tu stai	
He/She/It is	Lei/Lui/Egli è	He/She/It stays	Lei/Lui/Egli sta	

We are	Noi siamo	We stay	Noi stiamo	
You are	Voi siete	You stay	Voi state	
They are	Loro sono	They stay	Loro stanno	

Here are some examples of the "verbo essere".

I am a fan.	Io sono un tifoso.
She is a bit short.	Lei è piuttosto bassa.
The party is around nine.	La festa è intorno alla nove.
It is two in the morning.	Sono le due di mattina

We have described someone and talked about the time.

Now, let's see some examples of the "verbo stare".

You keep quiet.	Tu stai in silenzio.
She is crying.	Lei sta piangendo.

www.LearnLikeNatives.com

Be careful!	Stai attento!
They are unwell.	Loro stanno male.

Is everything clear? Don't worry! It will all become clear if you repeat it over and over again.

Alongside the verb "to be", the second most important verb in the Italian language is "to have" – "avere" –. It is an auxiliary and irregular verb that allows you to express numerous things: possessing something (literally or in a figurative way), communicate needs and desires, etc.

To have	**Avere**
I have	Io ho
You have	Tu hai
He/She/It has	Lei/Lui/Egli ha
We have	Noi abbiamo
You have	Voi avete

| They have | Loro hanno |

I have an appointment at eight.	Io ho un appuntamento alle otto.
It has big paws.	Ha grandi zampe.
We have a plan.	Noi abbiamo un piano.
They have a house by the lake.	Loro hanno una casa sul lago.

Are you looking forward to putting this into practice?

Emma: *Hi. I am Emma.*

Ciao. Io sono Emma.

David: *Nice to meet you. I am David.*

Piacere di conoscerti. Io sono David.

Emma: *Tell me, David. What do you like to do?*

Dimmi, David. Cosa ti piace fare?

David: *I enjoy sailing on weekends.*

Mi piace fare vela nel fine settimana.

Emma: *Do you have a boat?*

Hai una barca?

David: *Yes, I do. And what do you like to do?*

Si. E a te cosa piace fare?

Emma: *I have a dancing academy. I love to teach.*

Ho una scuola di danza. Io amo insegnare.

David: *Really? I have a niece. She loves to dance.*

Davvero? Io ho una nipote. Lei adora ballare.

Emma: *Great! How old is she?*

Fantastico! Quanti anni ha?

David: *She is 6 years old. Turns 7 in two weeks.*

Lei ha 6 anni. Ne compie 7 tra due settimane.

Emma: *I teach from 7. Maybe you could bring her.*

Io insegno a partire dai 7 anni. Magari potresti portarla.

David: *Awesome. I am sure she will love it.*

Stupendo. Sono certo le piacerà molto.

As you can see, it is very important to know how to conjugate the Present simple. Just keep practicing until you achieve a better understanding.

Chapter 5 – Have a look around

Now, have a look around the room and tell me what you see. What's all around you? For instance, I usually keep a bottle of water on my desk, and I always carry my mobile phone and wallet. In this chapter, we will learn the names of a few things that you will probably have in your house.

Clock	Orologio
My **clock** says it is late.	Il mio **orologio** dice che è tardi.

Orh-roh-loh-joh

Remember what we said at the beginning about punctuality? You will need a "orologio" to be always right on time.

Light	Luce
Turn the **light** on.	Accendi la **luce.**

Loo-ceh

Money	Soldi
Spend your **money** wisely.	Spendi i tuoi **soldi** con saggezza

Sohl-dee

Bed	Letto

www.LearnLikeNatives.com

| This **bed** is very comfortable. | Questo **letto** è molto comodo. |

Leh-toh

| Window | Finestra |
| That **window** points south. | Questa **finestra** si affaccia a sud. |

Fih-nehs-trah

| Water | Acqua |
| I want some **water**. | Voglio un pò di **acqua.** |

Ah-kwah

| Car | Auto |
| That is a nice **car.** | Quella è una bella **auto**. |

How-toh

| Bicycle | Bicicletta |

| I took your **bicycle.** | Ho preso la tua **bicicletta**. |

Bee-cee-kleh-tah

| Photo | Fotografia |
| I have your **photo** in my wallet. | Ho una tua **fotografia** nel mio portafoglio. |

Foh-toh-grah-fee-ah

| News | Notizie |
| Did you read the **news**? | Hai letto le **notizie**? |

Noh-tee-zee-ah

"Notizie" are very important to keep you informed. Let me give you a little advice. When preparing to visit another country, you should start reading local news sources from that place a couple of weeks before you get there. That will give you an insight into what is happening in the country and – why not – also some great talking points when you are speaking with locals.

| Bin | Cestino |
| I put it all in the **bin**. | Ho buttato tutto nel **cestino**. |

Chehs-tee-noh

Toothbrush	Spazzolino da denti
I need a new **toothbrush**.	Ho bisogno di un nuovo **spazzolino da denti**.

Spah-tzoh-lee-noh dah dehn-tee

Mirror	Specchio
That **mirror** looks dirty.	Quello **specchio** sembra sporco.

Speh-keeoh

Laptop	(Computer) portatile
You can use my **laptop**.	Puoi usare il mio **portatile**.

Kom-pooh-terh por-tah-tee-leh

Computer	Computer
That is my **computer**.	Quello è il mio **computer**.

Kohm-pooh-terh

Cellphone	(Telefono) cellulare

| I don't find my **cellphone**. | Non trovo il mio **cellulare**. |

Cheh-loo-lah-reh

Id	Documento
Please, let me see your **id**.	Per favore, mostrami un tuo **documento**.

Doh-cooh-mehn-toh

Driving license	Patente di guida
You look funny in your **driving license**.	Sei buffo sulla tua **patente di guida**.

Pah-tehn-teh dee gwih-dah

Wallet	Portafoglio
Did you find your **wallet**?	Hai trovato il tuo **portafoglio**?

Porh-tah-foh-lihoh

Are you ready to create your own list? How many of those things are there in your house? Ok, let us take an example to understand it better.

Nancy: *Honey! Do you have everything you need for camp?*

Tesoro! Hai preso tutto quello che ti serve per il campeggio?

Peter: *Yes, mom. I think so.*

Si, mamma. Penso di si.

Nancy: *Do you have your id and cellphone?*

Hai preso i documenti e il cellulare?

Peter: *Yes. I cannot find my toothbrush.*

Si. Ma non riesco a trovare il mio spazzolino da denti.

Nancy: *I saw it by the bathroom's mirror.*

L'ho visto nel bagno, vicino allo specchio.

Peter: *Thanks! Can I bring my laptop?*

Grazie! Posso portare il mio portatile?

Nancy: *To camp? No! Bring your wallet. You need that.*

In campeggio? No! Portati il portafoglio. Ne avrai bisogno.

Peter: *I need money, too.*

Ho anche bisogno di soldi.

Nancy: *It is on your bed.*

Sono sul tuo letto.

Peter: *Good. I also need water and a small bin.*

Perfetto. Mi servono anche acqua e un piccolo cestino.

Nancy: *A bin? Why?*

Un cestino? Perchè?

Peter: *For the food. Haven't you read the news? It's bear season.*

Per il cibo. Non hai letto le notizie? È la stagione degli orsi.

Nancy: *Really? Ok. Keep your light close to you, just in case.*

Davvero? Ok. Tieni sempre la torcia vicino a te, per sicurezza.

Peter: *Sure. Thanks, mom.*

www.LearnLikeNatives.com

Va bene. Grazie, mamma.

It is getting easier; I can feel it. I guarantee that if you follow the instructions and keep repeating our little lessons, you will make rapid progress and you'll be able to communicate fluently in Italian very soon. Feel free to go back to the previous chapters as many times as you like, all it takes sometimes is just a little something to jog your memory!

If you need help to count how many times you are repeating a sentence, move on to the next chapter: we are going to learn numbers next!

Chapter 6 – How far can you count?

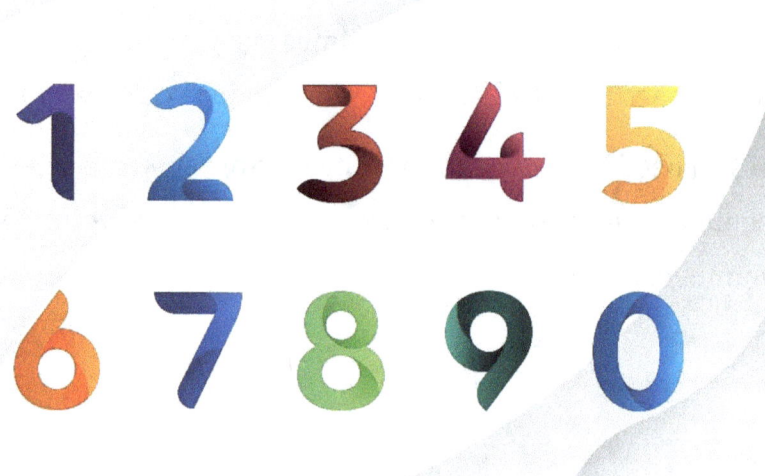

There are many nursery rhymes that help to introduce numbers even before a child understands numbers or how to count. It was probably through one of these songs that many of us learned numbers and measurements.

That is what we will learn in this chapter. Don't worry. You won't have to do any math!

www.LearnLikeNatives.com

When speaking in Italian, you will often need to use and understand numbers to express time, record dates and – of course – count. So, here is a table to help you memorize them:

		Pronunciation
One	Uno	Uh-noh
Two	Due	Doo-eh
Three	Tre	Treh
Four	Quattro	Kwua-troh
Five	Cinque	Cheen-kweh
Six	Sei	Seh-ee
Seven	Sette	She-teh
Eight	Otto	Oh-toh
Nine	Nove	Noh-veh
Ten	Dieci	Diheh-cee
Eleven	Undici	Oon-dee-cee

Twelve	Dodici	Doh-dee-cee
Thirteen	Tredici	Treh-dee-cee
Fourteen	Quattordici	Kwaht-tohr-dee-cee
Fifteen	Quindici	Kween-dee-cee
Sixteen	Sedici	Seh-dee-cee

As you can see, all the numbers from one to ten are specific words, and as such, you will have to learn it by heart. From eleven to sixteen, numbers are formed from the root of the digit (i.e. "un-") followed by ten ("-dici" instead than dieci).

For numbers from seventeen to nineteen, the order is reversed: the root -dici and then the unit:

Seventeen	Diciassette	Dee-chahs-seh-teh
Eighteen	Diciotto	Dee-cho-toh
Nineteen	Diciannove	Dee-chah-noh-veh

The same goes for numbers from 21 to 29. We just take the root number (venti) and add the unit.

Twenty	Venti	Vehn-tee
Twenty-one	Ventuno	Vehn-tooh-noh
Twenty-two	Ventidue	Vehn-tee-doo-eh
Twenty-three	Ventitrè	Vehn-tee-treh
Twenty-four	Ventiquattro	Vehn-tee-kwah-troh
Twenty-five	Venticinque	Vehn-tee-cheen-kweh
Twenty-six	Ventisei	Vehn-tee-sahy
Twenty-seven	Ventisette	Vehn-tee-seh-teh
Twenty-eight	Ventotto	Vehn-toht-oh
Twenty-nine	Ventinove	Vehn-tee-noh-veh

You may have already noticed that when the ten unit ends in a vowel (like in this case "venti") and you add a unit that begins with a vowel (i.e. "uno"), the first word loses its vowel. As a consequence, "venti" and "uno" make "ventuno".

www.LearnLikeNatives.com

Moreover, when a number ends in -tre, you will need to add an accent: -trè.

Thirty	Trenta	Trehn-tah
Thirty-one	Trentuno	Trehn-too-noh
Thirty-two	Trentadue	Trehn-tah-doo-eh
Forty	Quaranta	Kwah-rahn-tah
Fifty	Cinquanta	Cheen-kwahn-tah
Sixty	Sessanta	Seh-sahn-tah
Seventy	Settanta	Seh-tahn-tah
Eighty	Ottanta	Oh-tahn-tah
Ninety	Novanta	Noh-vahn-tah
One hundred	Cento	Chehn-toh
One thousand	Mille	Mee-leh

You can familiarize with numbers by repeating them to yourself over and over. It also helps if you count out loud.

Let's move on to ordinal numbers. As the name suggests, they tell the "order" of things. That way, we can make ranks, prioritize, and set dates. Awesome, uh?

First	Primo	Pree-moo
Second	Secondo	Seh-kohn-doh
Third	Terzo	Terh-tzoh
Fourth	Quarto	Kwarh-toh
Fifth	Quinto	Kwihn-toh
Sixth	Sesto	Sehs-toh
Seventh	Settimo	Seh-tee-moh
Eighth	Ottavo	Oh-tah-voh
Ninth	Nono	Noh-noh
Tenth	Decimo	Deh-chee-moh

As is the case with cardinal numbers, each of the first ten ordinal numbers has a distinct form. Form eleventh onward, ordinal numbers are formed by dropping the final vowel of the number and adding the suffix -esimo:

Eleventh	Undicesimo	Oon-dee-ceh-see-moh
Twelfth	Docicesimo	Doh-dee-ceh-see-moh
Thirteenth	Tredicesimo	Treh-dee-ceh-see-moh
Fourteenth	Quattordicesimo	Kwah-torh-dee-ceh-see-moh
Fifteenth	Quindicesimo	Kween-dee-ceh-see-moh

Let's now have a look at bigger numbers and the prefixes that will help us create even higher numbers.

Twentieth	Ventesimo	Vehn-teh-see-moh
Thirtieth	Trentesimo	Tren-teh-see-moh
Fortieth	Quarantesimo	Kwah-rahn-teh-see-moh

Fiftieth	Cinquantesimo	Cheen-kwahn-teh-see-moh
Sixtieth	Sessantesimo	Seh-sahn-teh-see-moh
Seventieth	Settantesimo	Seh-tahn-teh-see-moh
Eightieth	Ottantesimo	Oh-than-teh-see-moh
Ninetieth	Novantesimo	Noh-vahn-teh-see-moh
Hundredth	Centesimo	Chen-teh-see-moh
Thousandth	Millesimo	Mih-leh-see-moh

Now it's your turn? Try to cover the right side of the page. Can you work out the answers to the below?

21th	Ventunesimo
32th	Trentaduesimo
45th	Quarantacinquesimo

58th	Cinquattotesimo
64th	Sessantaquattresimo
79th	Settantanovesimo
83rd	Ottantatreesimo
95th	Novantacinquesimo
108th	Centoottesimo

Have you seen how easy it is to create higher ordinal numbers? I know it's not a competition, but why not try to get there first?

Chapter 7 – What did you want to be when you grew up?

"What did you want to be when you grew up?" How many times did someone ask you this question when you were a child? And how many times have you changed your answer?

When I was little, I wanted to be a scientist. Later on, I wanted to be a singer. Nowadays, I am a writer, but previously I have had different jobs. I have been a teacher, an electrician – honestly, not a very good one- and a chef.

We always need to remember that all professions are important. We need farmers to produce food of the highest quality, doctors to treat injuries and disease, artists to represent the beauty of the world around us, and so on.

Speaking of artists, this is a good word to start with.

Artist	Artista
Picasso was an **artist**.	Picasso era un **artista**.

Arh-tees-tah

You should always keep in mind that vowels like "a" are very open and clear in Italian. "A" is pronounced like the English word "ah!". "Artista"

Chef	Cuoco
I want to become a **chef**.	Voglio fare il **cuoco**.

Kwoh-coh

Construction worker	Muratore
My dad is a **construction worker**.	Mio papà è un **muratore**.

Mooh-rah-toh-reh

www.LearnLikeNatives.com

Firefighter	Pompiere
Being a **firefighter** is a risky job.	Fare il **pompiere** è un lavoro pericoloso.

Pom-peeh-eh-reh

Doctor	Dottore
The **doctor** will see you in 5 minutes.	Il **dottore** ti riceverà in 5 minuti.

Doh-toh-reh

Policeman	Poliziotto
A **policeman** came to our house.	Un **poliziotto** è venuto a casa nostra.

Poh-lee-tziho-toh

Teacher	Insegnante
That is my **teacher**.	Lei è la mia **insegnante**.

Ihn-seh-nyahn-teh

Actor/Actress	Attore/Attrice

Emma Stone is an **actress**.	Emma Stone è un'**attrice**.

Ah-toh-reh/Ah-tree-ceh

Banker	Banchiere
I am waiting for a **banker**.	Sto aspettando un **banchiere**.

Bahn-kee-eh-reh

Butcher	Macellaio
I am calling the **butcher** to order.	Sto chiamando il **macellaio** per ordinare.

Mah-cheh-lah-yoh

Dentist	Dentista
I have a great **dentist**.	Ho un **dentista** molto bravo.

Dehn-tees-tah

Driver	Conducente
My **driver** is very fast.	Il mio **conducente** va molto veloce.

Kon-doo-chen-teh

Are you making any progress?

Electrician	Elettricista
You need to call the **electrician**.	Devo chiamare l'**elettricista**.

Eh-leh-tree-cis-tah

Farmer	Contadino
My grandpa was a **farmer**.	Mio nonno faceva il **contadino**.

Kon-tah-dee-noh

Hairdresser	Parrucchiere
I have a great **hairdresser**.	Ho un bravo **parrucchiere**.

Pah-rooh-kihe-reh

Journalist	Giornalista
I will be a **journalist.**	Io farò il **giornalista**.

Jorh-nah-lihs-tah

Lawyer	Avvocato
My daughter is a **lawyer**.	Mia figlia è **avvocato**.

Ah-voh-kah-toh

Painter	Pittore
That **painter** did a good job.	Quel **pittore** ha fatto un buon lavoro.

Pee-toh-reh

There are plenty of professions but don't worry, we won't go through them all. Just few more words.

Politician	Politico
I want to be a **politician**.	Voglio diventare un **politico**.

Poh-lih-tee-coh

Psychologist	Psicologo
I am a **psychologist**.	Io sono **psicologo**.

Psi-koh-loh-go

Scientist	Scienziato

Scientists are addressing climate change.	Gli **scienziati** stanno affrontando il cambiamento climatico.

She-hen-tzah-toh

What did you want to be when you grew up? Let's learn few more words.

Plumber	Idraulico
I have to call the **plumber.**	Devo chiamare l'**idraulico**.

Ee-drau-lee-coh

Secretary	Segretaria
My **secretary** is on vacation.	La mia **segretaria** è in vacanza.

Seh-greh-tah-ree-ah

Shoemaker	Calzolaio
The **shoemaker** made a good job.	Il **calzolaio** ha fatto un buon lavoro.

Kal-zoh-lah-joh

Singer	Cantante
She's a great **singer**.	Lei è una brava **cantante**.

Kan-tan-teh

Waiter/Waitress	Cameriere/Cameriera
I'll call the **waiter**.	Chiamo il **cameriere**.

Ka-meh-riheh-reh/Ka-meh-riheh-rah

Writer	Scrittore
It is hard to be a **writer**.	È difficile diventare uno **scrittore**.

Skriht-toh-reh

Translator	Traduttore
I work as a **translator**.	Io lavoro come **traduttore**.

Tra-doo-toh-reh

Ready for a short dialogue?

Cris: *Hey! What do you have there?*

Ehi! Che cos'hai lì?

Layla: *It's a firefighter costume.*

È un costume da pompiere.

Cris: *Is November yet?*

È già Novembre?

Layla: *No! My son's school is going to have a "career day".*

No! La scuola di mio figlio sta organizzando una "giornata delle professioni".

Cris: *Oh, I see. I wanted to be a psychologist when I was nine.*

Oh, capisco. Io sognavo di diventare psicologo quando avevo nove anni.

Layla: *I wanted to be a teacher. We are always changing, right?*

Io volevo fare l'insegnante. Come cambiano le cose, vero?

Cris: Yeah. I also wanted to be a teacher when I was fourteen.

Si. Anche io volevo diventare professoresse quando avevo quattordici anni.

Layla: How did you decide to become a lawyer?

Poi come hai deciso di fare l'avvocato?

Cris: Well... you know. I was seventeen and wanted to change the world.

Beh... vedi. Avevo diciassette anni e volevo cambiare il mondo.

Layla: My son wants to be a farmer.

Mio figlio vuole fare il contadino.

Cris: Isn't his dad a politician?

Suo papà non fa il politico?

Layla: Yeah. He started as a journalist and then changed careers.

Si. Aveva iniziato come giornalista e poi ha cambiato carrierra.

Cris: Indeed. We are always changing.

È proprio vero. Cambiamo continuamente.

Now, repeat with me: "I wanted to be" -"Io volevo essere" and complete the sentence.

One of the first questions people ask to someone they have just meet is "What is your job?" which translates to "Che lavoro fai?". Thanks to what we have just learned in this unit, you are going to be ready for this conversation!

What next? Let's go to learn how to ask for directions.

Chapter 8 – Where are we going?

Being able to clearly tell where you want to go is very important, especially when traveling in another country. For this reason, the ability to communicate in simple situations such as asking for directions can make your life easier, in case of a SatNav failure or during a relaxing afternoon walk when you don't have your mobile with you.

Street	Strada
That is the main **street**.	Quella è la **strada** principale.

Strah-dah

Avenue	Viale
This is Liberazione **Avenue**.	Questo è il **Viale** della Liberazione.

Vihah-leh

Block	Quartiere/Isolato
We are going to the **block** party.	Stiamo andando alla festa di **quartiere**.

Kwuar-teeheh-reh / Ee-zoh-lah

Square	Piazza
The **square** should be a few blocks ahead.	La **piazza** dovrebbe essere qualche isolato più avanti.

Pihah-tzah

Are you pronouncing those vowels properly? Open vowels, remember?!

Building	Edificio
This **building** has 110 floors.	Questo **edificio** ha 110 piani.

Eh-dee-fee-choh

Monument	Monumento
This **monument** is 300 years old.	Questo **monumento** ha 300 anni.

Moh-nooh-mehn-toh

www.LearnLikeNatives.com

Hospital	Ospedale
The **hospital** is 5 minutes away.	L'**ospedale** dista 5 minuti da qui.

Ohs-peh-dah-leh

Corner	Angolo
The store is passing that **corner.**	Il negozio è dopo quell'**angolo**.

Ahn-goh-loh

Nearest	Più vicino
That is the **nearest** mall.	Quello è il centro commerciale **più vicino**.

Pihyou vih-chih-noh

Turn left	Girare a sinistra
You should **turn left** in two blocks.	Devi **girare a sinistra** tra due isolati.

Jih-rah-reh ah see-nihs-trah

Turn right	Girare a destra

| Let's **turn right** after this corner. | Dobbiamo **girare a destra** dopo l'angolo. |

Jih-rah-reh ah dehs-trah

| Go straight on | Continuare dritto |
| You only have to **go straight** on, and you will get there. | Ti basterà **continuare dritto** e ci arriverai. |

Kon-tee-noohah-reh dree-toh

| Go past | Oltrepassare |
| You have to **go past** the main street. | Devi **oltrepassare** la strada principale. |

Ohl treh-pah-sah-reh

| Crossroads | Incrocio |
| Take a left on the **crossroads.** | Svolta a sinistra all'**incrocio**. |

Ihn-croh-choh

Those phrases will take you wherever you desire! Are you ready to put into practice what we have just learned about directions?

John:	*¡Hey, sir! Good afternoon.*
	Salve, signore! Buon pomeriggio.
Vendor (Negoziante):	*What can I do for you?*
	Come posso aiutarti?
John:	*Can you tell me how I can get to the train station?*
	Puoi dirmi come raggiungere la stazione dei treni?
Vendor	*Sure. You have to go in that direction for three blocks.*
	Certo. Devi proseguire in quella direzione per tre isolati.
John:	*I have to go past the library?*
	Devo oltrepassare la biblioteca?
Vendor	*Yes. Then, you turn left and go for another five or six blocks.*
	Si. Poi, svolta a sinistra e prosegui per altri cinque o sei isolati.

John:	*Oh, I think I come from there. But I got confused at the crossroads.*
	Oh, credo di essere venuto da quella direzione. Ma ho fatto confusione all'incrocio.
Vendor	*Very usual. You have to take a left in the crossroads.*
	Succede spesso. Devi girare a sinistra all'incrocio.
John:	*Ok.*
	Va bene.
Vendor	*You will see a square. The station is in front.*
	Poi vedrai una piazza. La stazione è lì di fronte.
John:	*Thank you very much.*
	Grazie mille.
Vendor:	*Don't worry. Have a nice trip.*
	Non c'è problema. Buon viaggio.

Are you ready to go and explore a new place? Better hurry! "Survival 101" is coming.

Chapter 9 – Survival 101

Each chapter contains helpful information, but this is particularly important. We have already said that: sometimes things go wrong. Your child may feel unwell, you could twist an ankle while hiking, lose your passport.... things do happen. So it's better to be prepared, right?

I believe that this sentence, in particular, is fundamental for you:

| Do you speak English? | Parli inglese? |

Parh-lee een-gleh-she

It is a question you should always remember, as could make your life much easier.

| Where is the bathroom? | Dove posso trovare il bagno? |

Doh-veh poh-soh troh-vah-reh eel bah-nyoh

How can I get to this place?	Come posso andare in questo posto?

Koh-meh poh-soh ahn-dah-reh ihn kwehs-toh pohs-toh

Where is the nearest hospital?	Dove si trova l'ospedale più vicino?

Doh-veh see troh-vah l ohs-peh-dah-leh pihyou vih-chih-noh

Extremely important: "Dove si trova l'ospedale più vicino?".

When is the next flight?	Quando è il prossimo volo?

Kwuan-doh eh eel proh-sih-moh voh-loh

Who can I talk to about this problem?	Con chi posso parlare di questo problema?

Kon kee poh-soh parh-lah-reh dee kwehs-toh proh-bleh-mah

Where can I find a policeman?	Dove posso trovare un agente di polizia?

Doh-veh poh-soh troh-vah-reh uhn ahjehn-the dee poh-lih-tzih-ah

Though I hope you will never need this:

| Where is the embassy? | Dove si trova l'ambasciata? |

Doh-veh see troh-vah l ahm-bah-sciah-tah

| What do I need to visit…? | Cosa mi serve per visitare…? |

Koh-sah mee sehr-veh pehr vee-she-tah-reh

| Where can I find…? | Dove posso trovare …? |

Doh-veh poh-soh troh-vah-reh …

Oh, I really hope you won't need any of them. But better safe than sorry! Let's see a short dialogue now.

Harry: Hello, sir. How can I get to Pizzeria Pino, in Due Giugno Avenue?

Salve, signore. Come posso arrivare a Pizzeria Pino, in Viale Due Giugno?

Driver: I can take you, but is far. Is someone waiting for you? It's rush hour.

Posso portarti, ma è lontano. C'è qualcuno che ti aspetta? È l'ora di punta.

Harry: No. I think I left my passport there.

No. Credo di aver dimenticato lì il mio passaporto.

Driver: It will take us at least 40 minutes to get there.

Ci metteremo almeno 40 minuti per arrivarci.

Harry: Ok. Maybe I can call someone there.

Va bene. Magari posso telefonare.

Vendor: Good afternoon. Pizzeria Pino.

Buon pomeriggio. Pizzeria Pino.

Harry: Hello! My name is Harry Klein. I was there last night, and I think I left my passport.

Salve! Mi chiamo Harry Klein. Ero lì ieri sera, e penso di aver dimenticato il mio passaporto.

Vendor: One second, please. Do you remember where you were sitting?

Un attimo, per favore. Ti ricordi dove stavi seduto?

Harry: Yes. I was at the bar, by the corner.

	Si. Ero al bar, all'angolo.
Vendor:	*Ok. Give me a second.*
	Va bene. Dammi un momento.
Harry:	*Ok.*
	Ok.
Vendor:	*Yeah. I just consulted my coworkers, and they did not find anything. I am sorry.*
	Allora. Ho appena parlato con i miei colleghi e non hanno trovato nulla. Mi dispiace.
Harry:	*Thank you.*
	Grazie.
Driver:	*They didn't find it?*
	Non lo hanno trovato?
Harry:	*No. Where is the nearest police station?*
	No. Dov'è la stazione di polizia più vicina?
Driver:	*Don't you want to go to your embassy? It could be better.*

Non vuoi andare alla tua ambasciata? Sarebbe meglio.

Harry: Oh, yes. Where's the UK embassy?

Oh, giusto. Dov'è l'ambasciata del Regno Unito?

Driver: Actually, it is near from here. We will be there in a few minutes.

È proprio qui vicino. Saremo lì in pochi minuti.

What a nightmare to lose your passport abroad! I sincerely hope you will never have to use any of these phrases.

Now, let's move on to something less stressful. Shall we switch to colors?

Chapter 10 – What is the color of the sky?

I will tell you a secret: I love a wonderful view, and everywhere I go, I like to just lose myself gazing at the sky. I particularly love the sunset. I also like the sunrise, but I'm really not a morning person.

How many colors are there in the sky?

| Yellow | Giallo / Gialla |

My dress is **yellow**.	Il mio vestito è **giallo**.

Jahl-loh / Jahl-loh

Blue	Blu
The sky looks very **blue**.	Il cielo è **blu**.

Bloo

Red	Rosso / Rossa
I bought a **red** car.	Ho comprato un'auto **rossa**.

Rho-soh / Rho-sah

Purple	Viola
Those flowers are **purple**.	Quei fiori sono **viola**.

Vihoh-lah

Pink	Rosa
My daughter wants a **pink** gown.	Mia figlia vuole una vestaglia **rosa**.

Roh-sah

Green	Verde

| The fields look very **green** this year. | I campi sono molto **verdi** quest'anno. |

Verh-deh

| Orange | Arancione |
| I want an **orange** t-shirt. | Voglio una maglietta **arancione**. |

Ah-rahn-choh-neh

| Brown | Marrone |
| Your dog is **brown**. | Il tuo cane è **marrone**. |

Mah-roh-neh

| Grey | Grigio |
| **Grey** is a mixed color. | Il **grigio** è un colore misto. |

Grih-joh

| Black | Nero |
| **Black** is my favorite color. | Il **nero** è il mio colore preferito. |

Neh-roh

White	Bianco
I painted the walls **white**.	Ho dipinto le pareti di **bianco**.

Bee-ahn-coh

Fun fact: black and white are not colors. They represent, respectively, the absence of light and the lack of shadow.

Let's look at an example.

Lisa: Hey, honey! I need your help with something.

Ehi, dolcezza. Ho bisogno del tuo aiuto con una cosa.

Alex: Yes, love. What is it?

Certo, amore. Di che si tratta?

Lisa: We need to pick the colors for the house before we move.

Prima di trasferirci dobbiamo scegliere i colori per la casa.

Alex: Oh, true. What do you have in mind?

Oh, certo. Cosa avevi in mente?

Lisa: *I was thinking of a light blue for our room, with touches of yellow.*

Stavo pensando ad un blu chiaro per la nostra camera, con tocchi di giallo.

Alex: *Ok. What have you thought of the living room?*

Va bene. E che idee hai per la sala?

Lisa: *I am thinking of a combination of red and white walls.*

Sto pensando a una combinazione di pareti rosse e bianche.

Alex: *Do you think that my black chair will match?*

Pensi andrà bene con la mia poltrona nera?

Lisa: *Positive. And for the studio, I was looking for something more neutral.*

Certamente. E per lo studio, vorrei qualcosa di più neutro.

Alex: *By neutral you mean...?*

Cosa intendi per neutro...?

Lisa: *Earth colors. Like a light brown.*

Colori della terra. Come marrone chiaro.

Alex: *And the nursery?*

E per la cameretta?

Lisa: *Grey, with a purple wall.*

Grigio, con una parete viola.

Alex: *It sounds amazing. Thanks for planning all this.*

Sembra perfetto. Grazie per aver pianificato tutto.

Lisa: *Sure! I love it!*

Certo! Mi fa piacere!

What about you? Are you already planning to repaint your whole house? And for your dining room, would you like to go and buy some lanterns at an artisanal market in Venice? Imagine all the things you could do! First of all, however, we need to get there. Shall we do that?

www.LearnLikeNatives.com

Chapter 11 – So much to do, so much to see

Where do you dream of going? Personally, I love the mountains. I grew up in a village in the valley, with a stunning view of the mountains. I think maybe that's why I do love mountains so much! But anyway, enough about me. Now, imagine where you would like to go.

Travel	Viaggiare
She lost the scarf during her last **travel**.	Ha perso la sua sciarpa durante il suo ultimo **viaggio**.

Vihah-jah-reh

Ticket	Biglietto
I bought a two-way **ticket**.	Ho comprato un **biglietto** andata e ritorno.

Bee-liheh-toh

www.LearnLikeNatives.com

Airplane	Aereo
This **airplane** is very big.	Questo **aereo** è molto grande.

Ah-eh-rih-oh

Reservation	Prenotazione
He made a **reservation** for tonight.	Lui ha una **prenotazione** per questa notte.

Preh-noh-taht-zihoh-neh

Hotel	Hotel
I like this **hotel**.	Mi piace questo **hotel**.

Oh-tehl

Room	Camera
They need a double **room**.	Loro vogliono una **camera** doppia.

Cah-meh-rah

Key	Chiave
I lost my **key**.	Ho perso la **chiave**.

www.LearnLikeNatives.com

Kihah-veh

Passport	Passaporto
Can I see your **passport**?	Posso vedere il tuo **passaporto**?

Pah-sah-porh-toh

Taxi	Taxi
Let's take a **taxi**.	Prendiamo un **taxi**.

Tax-see

"Taxi" is the same both in Italian and in English.

Car rental	Noleggio auto
Where is the **car rental**?	Dove si trova il **noleggio auto**?

Noh-leh-joh how-toh

Bus	Autobus
We will take the **bus**.	Noi prenderemo l'**autobus**.

How-toh-boohs

Subway	Metropolitana

| The subway was out of service. | La **metropolitana** è fuori servizio. |

Meh-troh-poh-lih-tah-nah

| Train | Treno |
| I'll take the **train**. | Io prenderò il **treno**. |

Treh-noh

| Station | Stazione |
| That is the nearest **station**. | Quella è la **stazione** più vicina. |

Stah-tzioh-neh

| Theater | Teatro |
| This **theater** was remodeled 5 years ago. | Questo **teatro** è stato ristrutturato 5 anni fa. |

Teh-ah-troh

| Beach | Spiaggia |
| She wants to go to the **beach**. | Lei vuole andare in **spiaggia**. |

Spihah-jah

Mountain	Montagna
They want to climb that **mountain.**	Loro vogliono scalare quella **montagna.**

Mohn-tah-nyah

Island	Isola
Let's go to that **island**.	Andiamo su quell'**isola**.

Ee-zoh-lah

City	Città
Milan is a very big **city**.	Milano è una **città** molto grande.

Chih-tah

Are you ready? You know what's coming next!

Shaun: *I want to buy the tickets for our travel. Can we decide on something?*

Voglio comprare i biglietti per il nostro viaggio. Possiamo decidere qualcosa?

Vanessa: *Sure! Where do we want to go?*

Certo! Dove vogliamo andare?

Shaun: *Not another city. I want to rest.*

Nessun altra città. Voglio riposarmi.

Vanessa: *I agree. Do you remember that beautiful mountain that Lisa showed us? Cortina D'Ampezzo.*

Sono d'accordo. Ti ricordi quel bel posto di montagna che ci ha mostrato Lisa? Cortina D'Ampezzo.

Shaun: *Oh, sure. That cozy mountain house, right?*

Oh, certo. Quella casa di montagna tanto carina, giusto?

Vanessa: *Yes. That one.*

Si. Proprio quella.

Shaun: *That sounds great. Do you think it is available?*

Che bella idea. Pensi abbiamo disponibilità?

Vanessa: *On it!*

Ci guardo!

Shaun: *Remember to check for a view.*

Cerca di trovare qualcosa con una bella vista.

Vanessa: *I got the perfect room! It is beautiful.*

Ho trovato la stanza perfetta. È carinissima.

Shaun: *Great. I need our passports to buy the tickets. I'll get them.*

Fantastico. Ho bisogno dei passaporti per comprare i biglietti. Li prenderò io.

Vanessa: *Sure. I am excited!*

Perfetto. Non vedo l'ora!

So, are you getting excited?

Repeat with me: "voglio andare a" –I want to travel to-, and make it happen. Traveling is an amazing way to meet new people and discover beautiful places. In my opinion, traveling is growing up and you can never end it!

A spontaneous trip, a last-second vacation… these are usually the best things, the kind of stories you will remember forever. Some memories are just amazing!

And do you know what else I like when traveling? The food!

www.LearnLikeNatives.com

A Quick Message

Before we start the final chapter of this book.

"No one can whistle a symphony. It takes a whole orchestra to play it." –

H.E. Luccock

Do you want to be part of the orchestra of the Learning Italian community?

Here is how:

If you're enjoying this book, I would like to kindly ask you to leave a brief review on Amazon.

Reviews aren't easy to come by, but they have a profound impact in supporting my work. This way, I can keep creating new content to help the whole community at my very best.

www.LearnLikeNatives.com

I would be incredibly thankful if you could just take a minute to leave a quick review on Amazon, even if it's just a sentence or two!

It's that simple!

Thank you so much for taking the time to leave a short review on Amazon.

The community and I are very appreciative, as your review makes a difference.

Now, let's get back to learning Italian!

Chapter 12 – I am a bit hungry

Food is a language that everyone understands. Food talks about us, about culture, and lifestyle. If you visit a foreign country, you have to at least try the local cuisine.

If you ask my opinion, I strongly believe that Italy has given the world one of its great cuisines: there is nothing like that! It is viewed as a form of art by many. However, contrary to common belief, there is no such a thing as "Italian cuisine", as this it is in reality a collection of different regional cuisines. You should know that Italians are deeply proud of their food.

Even UNESCO has recognized the Mediterranean Diet (using fresh tomatoes, olive oil, and garlic) on a list of "Intangible Cultural Heritage of Humanity".

In the past centuries, a lot of Italians have emigrated, mainly to America, taking with them their culinary experience. Of course, coming in contact with different cultures widens their view and obliged them to make some changes to the original recipes.

I am sure that local people will love to tell you everything about their cuisine, but for now, let me just teach you a few basics words.

Let's start with breakfast.

Cappuccino	Cappuccino
A **cappuccino,** please.	Un **cappuccino** per favore.

Kah-pooh-cee-noh

I'm sure you are already familiar with this word. It is usually a breakfast drink, and no Italian would have one after 11am or with a meal.

Milk	Latte
I think this **milk** has gone bad.	Credo il **latte** sia andato a male.

Lah-the

Contrary to what happens in England, if you ask for a "latte" in Italy, you would be presented with a glass of milk. So be sure to use its full name: "Caffelatte" – literally coffee with milk.

Croissant	Cornetto
Breakfast includes **croissant** and cappuccino.	La colazione è **cornetto** e cappuccino.

Kohr-neh-toh

If you wish to sound like an Italian native, in the morning, you should go to the bar and ask for "cornetto e cappuccino". This is the typical Italian breakfast, a sweet treat.

Cake	Torta

| Have another slice of **cake**. | Prendi un'altra fetta di **torta**. |

Torh-tah

| Pancakes | Frittelle |
| These **pancakes** are fluffy. | Queste **frittelle** sono soffici. |

Free-the-leh

Hope you are getting hungry because it's time to go to a pizzeria:

| Pizza | Pizza |
| We are going out for a **pizza** tonight. | Usciamo a mangiare la **pizza** stasera. |

Peeh-tzah

| Tomato | Pomodoro |
| You only need a few **tomatoes**. | Ti serve solo qualche **pomodoro**. |

Poh-moh-dorh-roh

Basil	Basilico
I have a **basil** plant.	Ho una pianta di **basilico.**

Bah-zee-lee-koh

Do you know the story of the most popular pizza margherita? In 1889, an Italian chef created a dish for Queen Margherita. It was a dough base with tomatoes, mozzarella cheese and fresh basil. The ingredients were resembling the Italian flag.

As the years passed, many variations of this pizza started to become available, but be careful when you order a pizza in Italy. Ordering a Hawaiian pizza would be a great mistake! Italians are purist when it comes to food, and pineapple does not belong on pizza.

Pepperoni pizza	Pizza con il salame
I would like a **pepperoni pizza**.	Vorrei una **pizza** con il salame.

Peeh-tzah kohn eel sah-lah-meh

Peppers	Peperoni

| I've bought **peppers** and potatoes. | Ho comprato **peperoni** e patate. |

Peh-peh-roh-nee

Yes, you have got it right! I am sure you love pepperoni pizza, but if you ask for it in Italy, they will serve you a pizza with… peppers! If you want a pepperoni, you should order a "pizza con salame" or "diavola".

| Pasta | Pasta |
| Italians eat a lot of **pasta.** | Gli Italiani mangiano un sacco di **pasta**. |

Pah-stah

Pasta is an important part of the Italian cuisine. It comes in a wide range of shapes and lengths. The most popular are probably spaghetti, fusilli and:

| Lasagna | Lasagna |
| Lasagna is my favorite food. | Il cibo che preferisco è la **lasagna**. |

Lah-sah-nah

Meatballs	Poplette
We had **meatballs** for dinner.	Abbiamo mangiato **polpette** per cena.

Pohl-peh-teh

Now, this is probably the biggest Italian myth: In Italy, you will not find a dish called "spaghetti and meatballs". This is an American creation, and not an authentic Italian dish.

Similarly, the Bolognese sauce is most common in the US as in Italy, this only refers to the one produced in Bologna, while every region has its own kind of sauce. The proper name of this minced meat in tomato sauce is "ragù" (rah-gooh).

Also, Italians do not eat pasta with chicken.

Egg	Uova
She wants **eggs** and ham.	Lei vuole **uova** e prosciutto.

Woh-vah

Cheese	Formaggio

www.LearnLikeNatives.com

| I don't eat **cheese**. | Io non mangio **formaggio**. |

Forh-mah-joh

| Butter | Burro |
| French people love **butter**. | I Francesi amano il **burro**. |

Booh-roh

| Sandwich | Panino |
| We want five **sandwiches**. | Vogliamo cinque **panini**. |

Pah-nee-noh

Does it sound familiar? I am sure you have ordered a "panini" before. You should be aware that "panini" is plural and means sandwiches. If you only want one sandwich, make sure to order a "panino".

| Salad | Insalata |
| I want a Caprese **salad**. | Io vorrei un'**insalata** Caprese. |

Ihn-sah-lah-tah

Sausage	Salsiccia
We love **sausages** for breakfast.	A noi piace mangiare **salsiccia** a colazione.

Sal-sih-chah

Bread	Pane
I bought the **bread** this morning.	Ho comprato il **pane** questa mattina.

Pah-neh

Artisanal bread is a big thing in Italy, and if you enter a local bakery, you will find plenty of different types of bread. Very popular is also "bruschetta" (Brews-keh-tah): a cooked slice of bread topped with chopped tomatoes.

Ham	Prosciutto
The flavor of **ham** is delicious.	Il sapore del **prosciutto** è delizioso.

Proh-shoo-toh

Chicken	Pollo
That **chicken** is raw.	Quel **pollo** è crudo.

Poh-loh

Rice	Riso
The **rice** is ready.	Il **riso** è pronto.

Ree-zoh

Soup	Zuppa
This **soup** is hot.	Questa **zuppa** è calda.

Zooh-pah

Onion	Cipolla
I was chopping **onions**.	Stavo tagliando le **cipolle**.

Chih-poh-lah

Garlic	Aglio
You need to add **garlic** and stir.	Devi aggiungere **aglio** e mescolare.

Ah-lih-oh

Lemon	Limone

| These **lemons** look very nice. | Questi **limoni** sembrano molto buoni. |

Lee-moh-neh

| Orange | Arancia |
| I would like an **orange** juice, please. | Vorrei un succo di **arancia**, per favore. |

Ah-rahn-chah

| Peanut | Arachidi |
| I am allergic to **peanuts**. | Sono allergico agli **arachidi**. |

Ah-rah-kee-dee

"Arachidi" is an important one. It is, after all, one of the most common food allergies.

We are almost done with this first level!

Just one more conversation! Let's go!

Veronica: *I am hungry.*

Ho fame.

Karol: *Let's see. If you fancy something sweet, there are still some croissants from the breakfast.*

Vediamo. Se hai voglia di qualcosa di dolce, ci sono ancora dei cornetti dalla colazione.

Veronica: *Uhm... Not really. Do we have ham and cheese? I could use the bread to prepare a panini.*

Uhm... Non proprio. Abbiamo prosciutto e formaggio? Potrei usare il pane per preparare un panino.

Karol: *No. I could not go grocery shopping yesterday.*

No. Non sono andata a fare la spesa ieri.

Veronica: *It is fine. Maybe I could go to that pizza place, by the corner.*

Non c'è problema. Magari potrei andare a quel posto che fa la pizza, all'angolo.

Karol: *I don't think it is open yet.*

Non penso sia ancora aperto.

Veronica: *Oh… I will go to buy some chicken, then. Do you want anything?*

Oh… allora, vado a comprare del pollo. Ti serve altro?

Karol: *That sounds nice! Can you get me a salad?*

Buona idea! Puoi prendermi un'insalata?

Veronica: *Sure! What kind of salad would you like?*

Certo! Che tipo di insalata vuoi?

Karol: *Maybe a chicken Caprese salad.*

Magari una insalata caprese.

Veronica: *Sounds fine. I will come back soon.*

Va bene. Tornerò presto.

I hope it wasn't too difficult as food is very important. Do you agree?

Conclusion

Congratulations, you've made it! See, it wasn't too hard, was it?

As you realized by now, this wasn't a typical language book. If you tried and failed to learn Italian in the past, you now discovered a new approach, one that you can build on to take your Italian adventure to the next level. In going away from formal vocabulary and grammar lessons, together we shifted your focus from 'learning' Italian, to 'speaking' Italian. Two very different things!

More than just the "rules" of Italian grammar, today you have a sense of "the soul and music" of the Italian language. You built a truly solid foundation in Italian and, even if you don't realize it yet, you are now capable of navigating social situations, create connections, keep contacts, as well as make friends. As I mentioned at the start, what's the point in knowing grammatical rules if you can't order your own food!

I won't bore you with the reasons why being able to speak another language is a huge benefit for you. Or why Italian in particular will open a world of opportunities. I'm sure you're already convinced! But learning a new language is indeed a complex and rich experience, making this book a journey – your journey – into a new culture.

A beautiful culture you're now part of.

No one is ever 'ready', so get out there! Travel, read fiction and newspapers in Italian, watch films, eat Italian foods, make Italian friends, and immerse yourself in Italian-speaking culture. Sure, you'll make a few mistakes at first. But who cares! You can always go back through our lessons and keep building your confidence. I'm sure you'll get there in no time.

This is just the first volume of this series, all packed full of vocabulary and dialogs, covering essential, everyday Italian that will ensure you master the basics.

www.LearnLikeNatives.com

You can find the rest of the books in the series, as well as a whole host of other resources, at **LearnLikeNatives.com**. Simply add the book to your library to take the next step in your language learning journey. If you are ever in need of new ideas or direction, refer to our 'Speak Like a Native' eBook, available to you for free at **LearnLikeNatives.com**, which clearly outlines practical steps you can take to continue learning any language you choose.

A language should be lived, not just learned. So learn it, live it and, most importantly, enjoy it!

www.LearnLikeNatives.com

www.LearnLikeNatives.com

Learn Like a Native is a revolutionary **language education brand** that is taking the linguistic world by storm. Forget boring grammar books that never get you anywhere, Learn Like a Native teaches you languages in a fast and fun way that actually works!

As an international, multichannel, language learning platform, we provide **books, audio guides and eBooks** so that you can acquire the knowledge you need, swiftly and easily.

Our **subject-based learning**, structured around real-world scenarios, builds your conversational muscle and ensures you learn the content most relevant to your requirements. Discover our tools at *LearnLikeNatives.com*

When it comes to learning languages, we've got you covered!

www.ingramcontent.com/pod-product-compliance
Lightning Source LLC
Chambersburg PA
CBHW072203100526
44589CB00015B/2338